At Sylvan, we believe reading is one of life's most important and enriching abilities, and we're glad you've chosen our resources to help your child build this critically important skill. We know that the time you spend with your children reinforcing the lessons learned in school will contribute to their love of reading. This love of reading will translate into academic achievement. Successful readers are ready for the world around them, ready to do research, ready to experience the world of literature, and prepared to make the connections necessary to achieve in school and in life.

At Sylvan we use a research-based, step-by-step process in teaching reading that includes thought-provoking reading selections and activities. As students increase their success as readers they become more confident. With increasing confidence, students build even more success. Our Sylvan activity books are designed to help you to help your child build the skills and confidence that will contribute to your child's success in school.

Included with your purchase of this activity book is a coupon for a discount at a participating Sylvan center. We hope you will use this coupon to further your child's academic journey. To learn more about Sylvan and our innovative in-center programs, call 1-800-EDUCATE or visit www.SylvanLearning.com.

We look forward to partnering with you to support the development of a confident, well-prepared, independent learner.

The Sylvan Team

Published in the United States by Random House, Inc., New York, and in Canada by Random House of Canada Limited, Toronto.

www.tutoring.sylvanlearning.com

Producer & Editorial Direction: The Linguistic Edge
Writer: Christina Wilsdon
Cover and Interior Illustrations: Shawn Finley and Duendes del Sur
Layout and Art Direction: SunDried Penguin

First Edition

ISBN: 978-0-307-47951-8
ISSN: 2161-9832

This book is available at special discounts for bulk purchases for sales promotions or premiums. For more information, write to Special Markets/ Premium Sales, 1745 Broadway, MD 6-2, New York, New York 10019 or e-mail specialmarkets@randomhouse.com.

PRINTED IN THE UNITED STATES OF AMERICA

10 9 8 7 6 5 4 3 2 1

Sylvan
Learning sm

2nd Grade
Reading Roundup

Blender Blunder

What do you call a blend of two consonants? A **consonant blend**, of course

LOOK at the consonant blends in the blender. MATCH each blend with the right ending. FILL IN the blanks with the correct blends.

1. _____bl_____ ouse

2. _____cl_____ oud

3. _____br_____ ave

4. _____dr_____ ive

5. _____fl_____ oor

6. _____tr_____ iangle

Sort It Out

Some blends are made up of three consonant sounds. The letter "s" pops up a lot, as in *spread*, *square*, and *stroke*.

SORT the words. PUT the words into the lists.

square   screech   scram   street   squirm
stripe   spray   strike   splat   scream
squash   split   spread   spring   splash

spr
Spray

spread

spring

squ
squirm

squash

square

scr
screech

scram

scream

str
strike

street

stripe

spl
splat

split

splash

Herd That Word

Words sometimes end with consonant blends, as in *elf*, *pump*, and *bent*. Cowgirl Pearl is busy rounding up some correct blends at the end of words!

LOOK at the blend next to each fence. READ the words inside the fence. CIRCLE the word that ends with the correct blend.

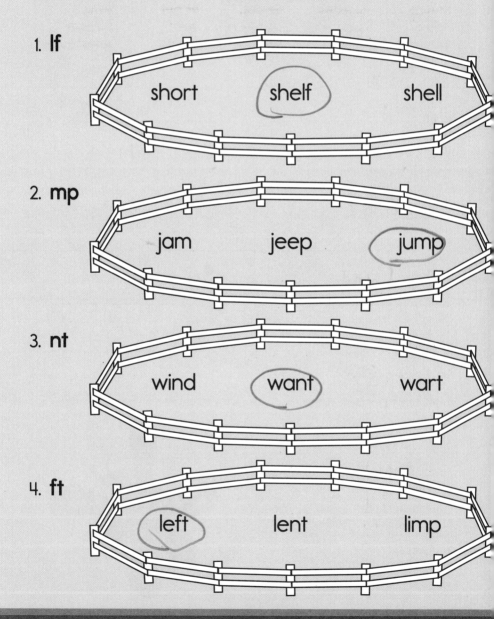

1. **lf**

short   shelf   shell

2. **mp**

jam   jeep   jump

3. **nt**

wind   want   wart

4. **ft**

left   lent   limp

Who Says?

Some consonant letters pair up to make a whole new sound, as in *cheer*, *fish*, and *thump*. We call these teams **consonant combos**. Check these chats for consonant combos. Each name shares a combo with one sentence.

READ each sentence. CIRCLE the consonant combos that repeat three times. MATCH sentences with names. DRAW lines between them.

1. She sells shells by the shore.

2. Your chubby chicken ate my cheese.

3. I think a thousand things a day.

4. You saw a white whale? Whatever.

5. Somebody threw three bananas through the window.

Theo

Whitney

Sheila

Thrasher

Chuck

Blender Blunder

LOOK at the consonant combos in the blender. MATCH each consonant combo with the right ending. FILL IN the blanks with the correct consonant combos.

1. __Ch__ eese
2. __Wh__ eel
3. __th__ under
4. __thr__ ead
5. __Sh__ ark

Follow That Sound

The letter "c" can sound like either **k** or **s**. Hard "c" sounds like **k**, as in *cold*. Soft "c" sounds like **s**, as in *cent*.

START at the arrow. DRAW a line along the path that is lined with words that start with a hard "c" to get to the cupcake.

Sort It Out

The letter "g" can be hard or soft too. Hard "g" sounds like the **g** in *goose*. Soft "g" sounds like **j**, as in *gem*.

SORT the words. PUT the words into the lists.

gab	general	giraffe	gobble	gentle	girl
giant	game	garden	goat	germ	ginger

Hard **g**   ### Soft **g**

What's This?

You can see them, but you can't hear them! They're letters in the silent consonant combos "kn," "wr," and "mb." The "k," "w," and "b" don't make a peep.

LOOK at each picture. READ the words next to it. CIRCLE the correct word.

HINT: *Shh!* The correct word has a silent consonant combo in it!

1. night   knight   knot

2. come   cob   comb

3. writer   water   wrong

4. nee   knee   kneel

Build It

The letter "e" is powerful when it's at the end of a word. It can change the word's sound by making its vowel long! *Hat*, for example, turns into *hate*.

ADD a final "e" to each word. FILL IN the blanks with the new words.

1. cut   +   e   = _____

2. dim   +   e   = _____

3. fin   +   e   = _____

4. fir   +   e   = _____

5. kit   +   e   = _____

6. mad   +   e   = _____

7. pin   +   e   = _____

8. plan   +   e   = _____

Follow That Sound

The letter "a" in *same* is a long vowel. But vowels can team up to sound like **a** too. These teams include "ei," "ai," and "ay."

START at the arrow. DRAW a line along the path filled with words that have a long **a** sound to get to the amazing brain.

Long E, It Seems

Blank Out!

See an "e," "ea," "ee," or "ey," and you may hear long **e**!

READ the sentences. FILL IN the blanks with long **e** words from the word box.

HINT: The correct word rhymes with a word next to it.

| sheep | sneak | neat | honey | seal | me |

1. Fish is a very good _____ meal.

2. You be _____ and I'll be you!

3. A clean chair is a _____ seat.

4. Bo Peep and her sisters all keep

   _____.

5. Where is all the money, _____?

6. I saw the movie early because I got

   a _____ peek.

Sound Search

Long i can be spelled "ie," "igh," and "y." Listen for it in *die*, *tight*, and *July*.

READ the story. CIRCLE words with the long i sound. FILL IN the blanks with the words.

Chef Toasty cooked all night long to bake the perfect pie. Just as the sky grew light, he put it on a high shelf. "My delight," he sighed. Chef shooed away a fly. Then he lay down for a nap. But a sly fox sneaked in a window. He grabbed the treat and ran. "Alas," cried Chef. Would he bake a new one? He could try.

_____   _____

_____   _____

_____   _____

_____   _____

_____   _____

Herd That Word

Oh, give me a home. . . . Cowgirl Roma goes where long **o** roams! It can be spelled "o," "oa," or "ow."

LOOK at the spelling of the long **o** sound next to each fence. READ the words inside the fence. CIRCLE the word that has the correct spelling of long **o**.

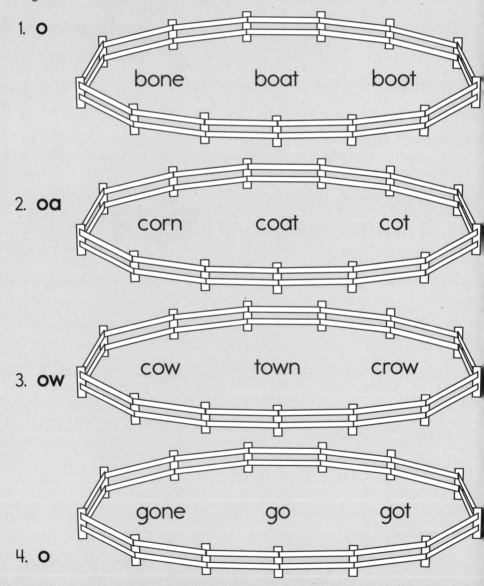

1. **o**

bone   boat   boot

2. **oa**

corn   coat   cot

3. **ow**

cow   town   crow

gone   go   got

4. **o**

What's This?

Hey, you! Long u can be spelled "u," "ew," "ue," and "ui." Examples are *music*, *chew*, *fuel*, and *fruit*.

LOOK at each picture. READ the words next to it. CIRCLE the correct word.

HINT: The correct word for each picture has a long **u**.

1. mule   mole   mill

2. stow   stew   stump

3. glow   goo   glue

4. just   joust   juice

Sort It Out

The letter "r" is the boss of vowels. It changes their sounds. Check out bossy "r" at work in "er," "ir," and "ur," as in *her*, *fir*, and *blur*.

SORT the words. PUT the words into the lists. WRITE them on the blanks.

first	burp	dinner	fur	dirt	curl
herd	bird	paper	turn	germ	girl

er

_____

_____

_____

_____

ir

_____

_____

_____

_____

ur

_____

_____

_____

_____

What's This?

he letter "r" can make vowels say **or** even if they're spelled with an "ar,"
or," "ore," or "our." Some examples are *wart, porch, more,* and *pour.*

OOK AT each picture. READ the words next to it. CIRCLE the correct word.

1. weird   award   word

2. horse   hours   house

3. cork   chore   core

4. for   fur   four

Herd That Word

The letter "r" makes "air," "are," and "ear" sound like **air** in many words, as in *fair*, *care*, and *tear*. Help Cowgirl Clair rope 'em!

LOOK at the spelling next to each fence. READ the words inside the fence. CIRCLE the word that has the correct spelling.

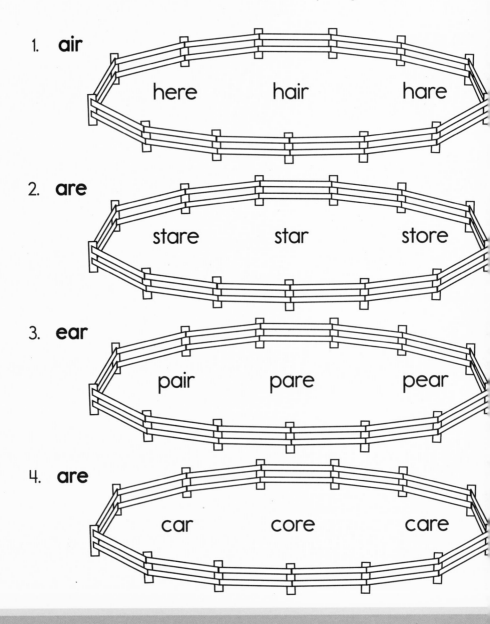

1. **air**

   here   hair   hare

2. **are**

   stare   star   store

3. **ear**

   pair   pare   pear

4. **are**

   car   core   care

What's This?

Sometimes letters just glide together to make a new vowel sound. The pairs "oi" and "oy," for example, make the sound **oy** as in *join* and *joy*.

LOOK AT each picture. READ the words next to it. CIRCLE the correct word.

1. buy   boy   boil

2. nose   knees   noise

3. eel   oil   ail

4. toy   toil   toe

Herd That Word

Yow! Cowgirl Wow is out to pounce on "ou" and "ow"! Both spellings can sound like **ow**.

LOOK at the spelling of the **ow** sound next to each fence. READ the words inside the fence. CIRCLE the word that has the correct spelling.

1. **ow**

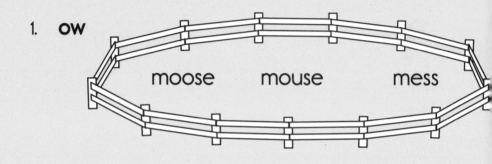

moose   mouse   mess

2. **ou**

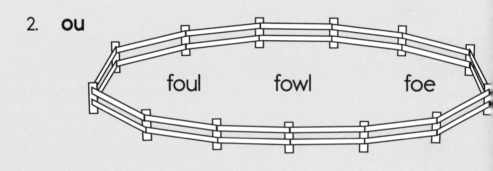

foul   fowl   foe

3. **ou**

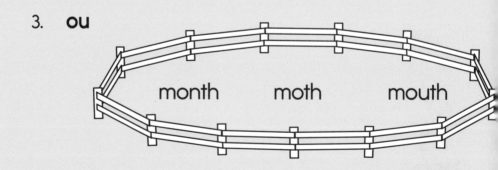

month   moth   mouth

Yo, Poet!

You go "moo" like a cow when you say the **oo** sound in *moon*. But "oo" can also sound like the **oo** in *book*. We'll call them the "Goo **oo**" and the "Good **oo**."

READ the poem. FILL IN the blanks with **oo** words from the word box.

good	Shoo	zoo	moose
room	drool	zoom	goose

There is a creature in my _____.

1

It likes to run and zip and _____.

2

It has feathers like a _____

3

And antlers like a big brown _____.

4

You might think that this is cool.

But you should see it drip and _____!

5

It doesn't smell _____. It belongs

6

in a _____.

7

But it won't go when I tell it, "_____!"

8

What's This?

You can hear an **aw** sound in words spelled with "aw." But the "a" in "al" and "all" sometimes says **aw** too! Examples are *straw*, *walk*, and *wall*.

LOOK at each picture. READ the words next to it. CIRCLE the correct word.

1. bawl   ball   bale

2. yawn   yarn   yen

3. hank   hunk   hawk

4. chick   check   chalk

You've Got Mail

Speedy speaking means losing letters! Squash *I* and *am* together and you get *I'm*. *You* and *will* make *you'll*. *Do* plus *not* make *don't*. Words like this are called **contractions**.

LOOK at the contractions in the word box. FILL IN the blanks with the right ones. You can use each contraction only once.

isn't	I'm	You're	wasn't	who's
Here's	it's	she's	I'll	what's

_____ not going to believe me,

1

but _____ true! My family is going

2

to the moon! Seriously. _____ the

3

plan: _____ going to build a rocket.

4

Guess _____ the pilot? My sister!

5

I _____ going to bring her, but

6

_____ the only driver. She says it

7

_____ going to work. _____

8   9

show her! So, _____ up with you?

10

Beat It!

Sort It Out

Pup is a word with one beat. *Puppy* has two beats. These beats are **syllables**. Most of the time, a syllable has a vowel in it.

COUNT the syllables in these words. SORT the words. PUT the words into the lists.

somebody	princess	bib	machinery
wonderful	yank	seventeen	cookie
armadillo	troublemaker	monster	wise

One Syllable

_____

_____

_____

Two Syllables

_____

_____

_____

Three Syllables

_____

_____

_____

Four Syllables

_____

_____

_____

Break It Up

SPLIT each word into syllables. FILL IN the blanks so that a dot sits between each syllable.

1. bulldozer = _____ • _____ • _____

2. crocodile = _____ • _____ • _____

3. fearful = _____ • _____

4. hamster = _____ • _____

5. basketball = _____ • _____ • _____

6. chipmunk = _____ • _____

7. Triceratops = _____ • _____ • _____ • _____

8. Apatosaurus =

____ • ____ • ____ • ____ • ____

Break It Up

A **prefix** is a letter or group of letters added to the beginning of a word. It changes a word's meaning. The prefixes "dis-" and "un-" swap a word's meaning. "Un-" turns *fair* into *unfair*. "Dis-" turns *respect* into *disrespect*. See what happens when you chop off these words' prefixes.

SPLIT each word. FILL IN the blanks with the prefix and the word.

1. unzip = _____ + _____

2. disagree = _____ + _____

3. disobey = _____ + _____

4. unreal = _____ + _____

5. disappear = _____ + _____

6. untie= _____ + _____

7. untidy = _____ + _____

8. dislike= _____ + _____

You've Got Mail

A **suffix** is a letter or group of letters added to the end of a word. A suffix can change a word's meaning a little or a lot. Adding "-er" or "-est," for example, makes *tall* even *taller* until it's the *tallest*.

LOOK at the suffixes in the word box. FILL IN the blanks with the right suffixes. You can use suffixes more than once.

-er	-est	-ed	-ing	-y	-ly

Today will be the weird_____ day ever. We're

visit_____ Aunt Rose. She has a very stink_____ pig

for a pet. Last time it chew_____ on my foot. Uncle

Al is meet_____ us there. He's even weird_____

than Aunt Rose. He lives in the world's dark_____

house. It's creep_____ and awful_____ cold, too!

Strange_____, he hasn't turn_____ on the heat

since 1969. Just think_____ about it makes me

feel cold_____.

Build It

ADD the words and suffixes. FILL IN the blanks with the new words.

1. rest + ing = _____

2. glad + ly = _____

3. blue + bird = _____

4. day + dream = _____

5. pre + heat = _____

6. mis + spell = _____

7. itch + y = _____

8. sick + est = _____

Answers

Page 2
1. blouse   2. cloud
3. brave   4. drive
5. floor   6. triangle

Page 3
spr: spray, spread, spring
squ: square, squash, squirm
scr: screech, scram, scream
str: stripe, strike, street
spl: split, splat, splash

Page 4
1. shelf   2. jump
3. want   4. left

Page 5
1. She, shells, shore→ Sheila
2. chubby, chicken, cheese→ Chuck
3. think, thousand, things→ Theo
4. white, whale, Whatever→ Whitney
5. threw, three, through→ Thrasher

Page 6
1. cheese   2. wheel
3. thunder   4. thread
5. shark

Page 7

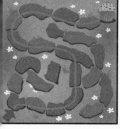

Page 8
Hard g: gab, goat, girl, game, garden, gobble
Soft g: gentle, general, germ, ginger, giraffe, giant

Page 9
1. knight   2. comb
3. writer   4. knee

Page 10
1. cute   2. dime
3. fine   4. fire
5. kite   6. made
7. pine   8. plane

Page 11

Page 12
1. seal   2. me
3. neat   4. sheep
5. honey   6. sneak

Page 13
night, pie, sky, light, high, my, delight, sighed, fly, sly, cried, try

Page 14
1. bone   2. coat
3. crow   4. go

Page 15
1. mule   2. stew
3. glue   4. juice

Page 16
er: dinner, germ, herd, paper
ir: bird, dirt, first, girl
ur: burp, curl, fur, turn

Page 17
1. award
2. horse
3. core
4. four

Page 18
1. hair   2. stare
3. pear   4. care

Page 19
1. boy   2. noise
3. oil   4. toy

Page 20
1. mouse   2. fowl
3. mouth

Page 21
1. room   2. zoom
3. goose   4. moose
5. drool   6. good
7. zoo   8. Shoo

Page 22
1. ball   2. yawn
3. hawk   4. chalk

Page 23
1. You're   2. it's
3. Here's   4. I'm
5. who's   6. wasn't
7. she's   8. isn't
9. I'll   10. what's

Page 24
One Syllable: bib, wise, yank
Two Syllables: cookie, monster, princess
Three Syllables: seventeen, somebody, wonderful
Four Syllables: armadillo, machinery, troublemaker

Page 25
1. bull · doz · er
2. croc · o · dile
3. fear · ful
4. ham · ster
5. A · pat · o · saur · us
6. chip · munk
7. Tri · cer · a · tops
8. bas · ket · ball

Page 26
1. un + zip
2. dis + agree
3. dis + obey
4. un + real
5. dis + appear
6. un + tie
7. un + tidy
8. dis + like

Page 27
Today will be the **weirdest** day ever. We're **visiting** Aunt Rose. She has a very **stinky** pig for a pet. Last time it **chewed** on my foot. Uncle Al is **meeting** us there. He's even **weirder** than Aunt Rose. He lives in the world's **darkest** house. It's **creepy** and **awfully** cold, too! **Strangely**, he hasn't **turned** on the heat since 1969. Just **thinking** about it makes me feel **colder**.

Page 28
1. resting   2. gladly
3. bluebird   4. daydream
5. preheat   6. misspell
7. itchy   8. sickest